A CLEAN SKY:

THE GLOBAL WARMING STORY

Robyn C. Friend
and
Judith Love Cohen

ILLUSTRATIONS:
David A. Katz

Editing:
Lee Rathbone

Cascade
Pass, Inc.
www.CascadePass.com

Published by Cascade Pass, Inc.
4223 Glencoe Avenue, Suite C-105
Marina del Rey, CA 90292-8801
Phone: (310) 305-0210
Web Site: http://www.CascadePass.com
Printed in China by South China Printing Co. Ltd

A Clean Sky: The Global Warming Story was written by Robyn C. Friend and Judith Love Cohen, designed and illustrated by David Katz, and edited by Lee Rathbone.

This book is one of a series that emphasizes the environment and the value of preserving it by depicting what real people are doing to meet the challenges.

Other books in the series include:
A Clean Sea: The Rachel Carson Story

Library of Congress Cataloging-in-Publication Data

Friend, Robyn C., 1955-
    A clean sky : the global warming story / Robyn C. Friend and Judith Love Cohen ; illustrations, David A. Katz.
    p. cm. – (Cascade Pass's environmental series)
Includes bibliographical references and index.
    ISBN 1-880599-81-3 (pbk. : alk. paper) – ISBN 1-880599-82-1 (hard cover : alk. paper)
    1. Global warming–Environmental aspects–Juvenile literature. 2. Climatic changes–Environmental aspects–Juvenile literature. I. Cohen, Judith Love, 1933- II. Katz, David A. (David Arthur), 1949- ill. III. Title. IV. Series.
QC981.8.G56F785 2007
363.738'74–dc22
                                                  2007019371

Introduction

Scientists today worry that the *climate* of our planet, the Earth, is changing in a way that will have bad effects on human, animal, and plant life. This is one of our biggest challenges now, and in the coming decades. We need to figure out what is causing the change, and what we can do to find a safer course.

This book tells the story of the global warming challenge, and some of the things we all can do to meet it.

This is the second book in Cascade Pass's environmental series dedicated to our planet Earth's resources – the oceans, the skies, the rainforests, the deserts… all those special environments that are shared by varieties of animals and plants – and to those whose efforts have protected them. *A Clean Sky: The Global Warming Story* discusses the possible dramatic changes to the Earth's climate, and how we can reduce this impact.

A Clean Sky: The Global Warming Story

Some days are filled with little problems: you lose a quarter from your pocket, you break a dish in the kitchen, you can't do your homework, you're coming down with a cold, and what do your friends tell you? "Tomorrow, the sun will come up and everything will be alright." And of course, the Earth turns on its axis, the sun rises in the East, and the new day is beautiful.

Some days are very frightening: a fire burns in a house down the street, lightning strikes a power pole, a monsoon destroys a fishing village, a flu epidemic hits. When we hear about these things, we may get frightened; but even if we are frightened, we know that the bad things are happening in just one small area, and it probably won't continue, or spread. These chance happenings are usually unexpected.

But what if I told you that there might be something unhealthy out there that we can see happening, that we can measure the potential effects, and that it could force many people to make drastic changes in where and how they live? And what if I told you that people are making plans to fight the bad effects, and that *you* can help?

This potential danger is caused by global climate change. First, what do we mean by "climate change"? Well, you've probably heard of "ice ages," those periods when much of the Earth was covered with snow and ice. These ice ages were separated by periods of warmer climate. The climate on Earth has changed over the years, sometimes gradually, sometimes rapidly.

Scientists think that these global warmings and coolings may have been caused by small changes in the amount of sunlight that the Earth receives, and also by erupting volcanoes.

Climate is all about the sun, and the effect it has on water and temperature on our planet. Water exists in three states: as a solid (ice, snow), as a liquid (rain), and as a vapor (humidity in the air, clouds, steam).

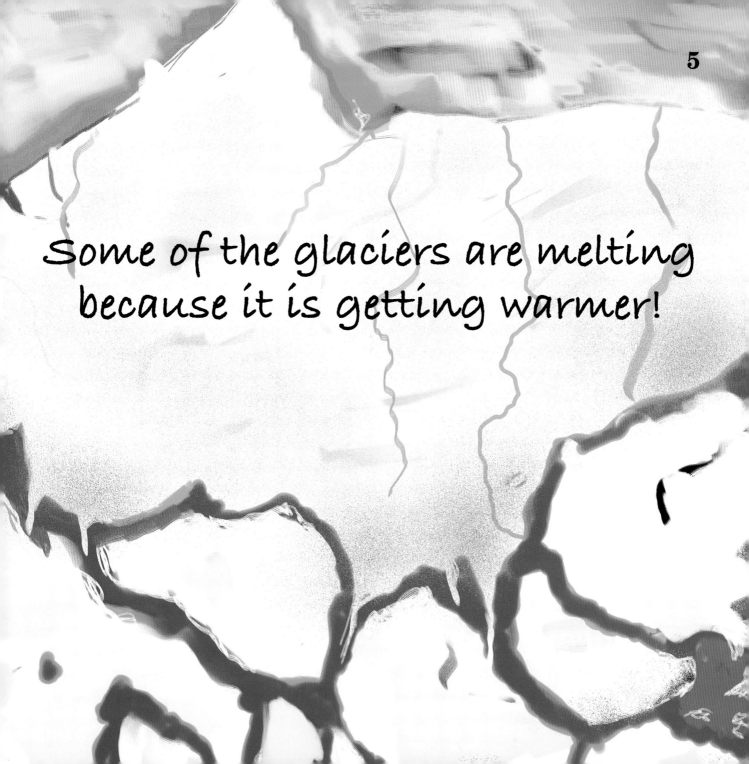

Some of the glaciers are melting because it is getting warmer!

Our climate seems to be getting warmer, and scientists now believe this is in part because of human activity.

How could people contribute to global warming? About 200 years ago, humans developed new technologies: instead of having only wood to burn for fuel, we learned how to burn *fossil fuels*, like coal and oil. As more humans burn these fuels, they put more of something called *Greenhouse Gases* in the atmosphere.

What is a greenhouse? A greenhouse is a glass house where plants are grown. The glass lets in the sunlight, but then keeps the sun's warmth from radiating back out.

What are greenhouse gases? In the 1800s, scientists first recognized that the atmosphere acted something like the glass in a greenhouse. The main greenhouse gas in the atmosphere that does this is water vapor, and the second most important greenhouse gas is *carbon dioxide*.

Carbon dioxide is produced when we exhale. We breathe in oxygen, we breathe out and there it is! All animals breathe in and out, exhaling *carbon dioxide*.

Plants and trees use carbon dioxide in their growing processes, removing it from the air.

So, what can we do? The most obvious answer is to plant more trees, cut down fewer trees, and stop creating more carbon dioxide than the plants and trees can use.

One way to put less carbon dioxide into the air is to use energy sources that produce little or no carbon dioxide, such as **solar power, wind power and natural gas.**

The energy of the sun can heat water, through a process called *passive solar heating*. Solar panels on rooftops let the sun heat water. Through the use of *photovoltaic cells*, the energy of the sun can be converted to electricity, and used in our homes, cars, and offices.

The sun also causes air in our atmosphere to move, creating wind. For a long time people have been using the blowing of the wind to run machinery like windmills to crush grain or pump water. Now we can use wind power to convert the energy of the wind into electricity.

The power of the wind
can be turned into
electricity and
turn on a light bulb!

Natural gas is a fossil fuel, like oil and coal, but burning it creates much less carbon dioxide than burning either oil (about 30% less) or coal (about 45% less). Natural gas is usually found in the same places as coal and oil. At one time, people drilling for oil just burned off the natural gas. Now we use it for heating and cooking, and as a source of electricity through gas *turbines*.

The fossil fuels are called *hydrocarbons,* because they consist of hydrogen and carbon. When hydrocarbons are burned for fuel, the hydrogen binds with oxygen in the air to form water vapor, and the carbon binds with the oxygen to form carbon dioxide. Thus the more motors that are run as a result of increased industrial development, the more carbon dioxide goes into the atmosphere. If, at the same time, more forests are cut down, then less carbon dioxide is being removed by plant life.

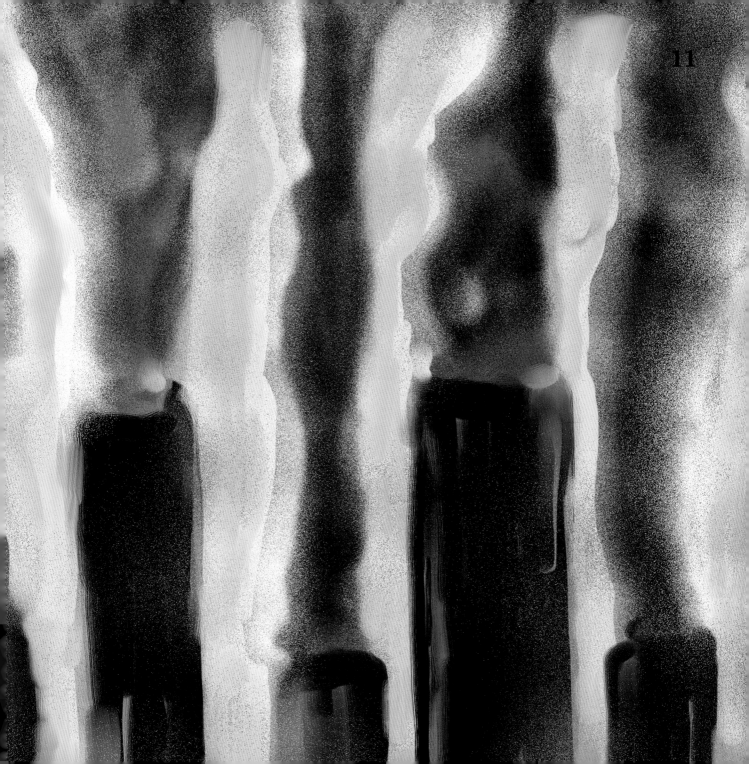

Now there's a new way of using energy that puts less carbon dioxide into the atmosphere: it's a process called **Carbon Capture and Geological Storage**. This new process has two parts. First, instead of letting the carbon dioxide escape into the Earth's atmosphere when the fuel is burned, chemists separate much of the carbon dioxide from the fuel before it is burned, and then store it in the pore-spaces (tiny, naturally-formed, holes) of the right kind of rock, deep underground. Second, the hydrogen that is left over is used to provide clean low-carbon energy.

Here's how it works: The process starts with a fossil fuel, like oil or coal. When these fuels are heated to a high temperature and then highly pressurized, the fuel turns into a gas. This gas is then cleaned to remove ingredients that cause smog, like sulfur. What is left are carbon dioxide and hydrogen.

Hydrogen

Oxygen

Water

Where does the hydrogen come from?

Carbon

Fossil
Fuel

Carbon
Dioxide

It's kind of like when you separate an egg for cooking. You want only the egg white for your angel food cake, not the egg yolk or the shells. So you separate the whites from the yolks, and strain the whites to remove the egg shells. Then you can save the egg yolks for another recipe, and beat the whites for your cake.

In the carbon separation and storage process, just like separating the eggs for your cake, we want to keep only the hydrogen, not the carbon dioxide. So the carbon dioxide is separated from the hydrogen, then compressed, and pumped through a pipeline to where it can be stored safely in the rocks.

Separating
the egg white
and yolk

The best kinds of rocks for storing the separated-out carbon dioxide are deep saline (salt water) rock formations, and also the kinds of rocks where we already find oil and natural gas. These rocks act like a sponge, and soak up the carbon dioxide and keep it in their pores.

In some of these rocks, carbon dioxide already occurs naturally, and has been locked into the rock for millions of years. In other geological formations, like volcanoes, geysers, and where naturally fizzy mineral waters come from, the carbon dioxide has leaked out. Scientists know why some rock leaks and some doesn't, so they know how to choose the right kind of rock to keep the carbon dioxide stored underground.

The second part of the process is to use the hydrogen left over from the separation of the carbon. This hydrogen gets used in a specially-designed power plant to generate electricity in a way that emits only a very small amount of carbon dioxide. This power plant uses the burning of the hydrogen to push turbines that create electricity, in the same way that natural gas-powered electricity plants do.

Turbines use fuel to make electricity.

But can we really do this? Some power and energy companies say: "Yes!" They have been storing carbon dioxide underground for more than 30 years to get more oil out of old oil wells, so we know it is possible to store the carbon dioxide safely and securely. Also, people already store natural gas underground in the same kind of porous rock formations. These projects show that gas can be stored safely and securely in these geological formations.

And the hydrogen will drive turbines similar to those turbines that have used natural gas to generate electricity in the same way and have been in use for decades.

In 2005, some innovative energy companies began to design the first large-scale projects using this process to generate clean electricity from fossil fuels. And they are planning to build them here in the USA and other countries.

These energy facilities will take a fossil fuel called petroleum coke (which is a byproduct of the oil refining process and has nothing to do with a soft drink!), and separate the carbon dioxide from it through safe and proven chemical processes.

Next they will pump the carbon dioxide deep into porous rock formations under the ocean where it can't escape into the atmosphere. They will then use the hydrogen left over from the separation process to fuel a power plant that will turn the turbines and generate clean "hydrogen power," electricity.

Separating the carbon dioxide from the hydrogen fuel.

The goal of one project in the USA includes: generating 500 megawatts of electricity. That's enough electricity to power 325,000 American homes with much lower emissions than if they burned just oil or coal.

A project of this size in the USA will capture and store up to 90% of its carbon dioxide underground totaling about 5 million tons of carbon dioxide per year. **That's 5 million tons of greenhouse gases that won't get into the atmosphere!**

The petroleum coke is available from the nearby refineries, so they will be using locally-generated fuel, instead of trucking it to the plant from somewhere far away.

Bringing the electricity to your home.

Power plants like this will accelerate the development of the hydrogen energy technologies and help to show that hydrogen power is a commercial alternative to the power generation we now use.

Hydrogen fuel turbines will be in operation, carbon capture methods will be used, and the technology to make and separate the hydrogen gas also will be demonstrated.

Moving Forward!

A Clean Sky and *YOU!*

What can you do?

First you need to learn more about the things we talked about: climate, the changes in the world around you, what affects your community and your environment. You need to read, to observe, to pay attention, and maybe look up things that sound interesting.

You need to ask questions, pay attention to the answers you get, and then search for more answers on your own.

In addition to using alternative energy to generate clean power, there are lots of things **you** can do to help decrease the amount of carbon dioxide we add to the atmosphere.

Learn About
the Environment

Be a part of the solution.

There are lots of things *you* can do to help decrease the amount of carbon dioxide we add to the atmosphere.

Some simple things are to save energy at home by using more energy-efficient lights; insulating your house so you need less energy to keep it a comfortable temperature inside; switch to energy-efficient appliances; reuse more things instead of throwing them away; and recycle glass, cans, plastic, and paper.

But **a very special** way for you to help is to become a scientist or an engineer, and help figure out how much warmer the climate will become if we don't slow it, what people can do to adapt to a warmer climate, or even possibly how to slow the warming trend.

Working
on Solutions!

There are also a number of energy technologies that if implemented may be able to slow, stop, or even reverse current trends in addition to using alternative energy to generate clean power. These strategies include improving the fuel efficiencies of cars, decreasing the number of miles traveled by cars, using power effectively in all buildings, producing electricity more efficiently, switching from coal to natural gas to generate electricity, capturing and storing carbon emissions from electricity plants, producing hydrogen from fossil fuels, increasing wind electricity capacity, installing more solar electricity capacity, using solar panels to produce hydrogen for fuel cells, increasing ethanol production, eliminating tropical deforestation, and using farming methods that conserve the soils.

And looking for new strategies that we haven't even thought of yet.

Looking for new ideas!

Future Goals:

Hydrogen and carbon separation technology has enormous potential. This could be the perfect solution to both our current dependence on oil and the carbon dioxide that other energy sources produce. We can create hydrogen from coal, sludge, and similar products. We can use hydrogen fuel turbines to generate electric power. We can capture and store the carbon dioxide. But hydrogen technology is new and being developed. We need to perfect the process.

Power plants like the one in California and others to come will accelerate the development of the hydrogen energy technologies and help to show that hydrogen power is a commercial alternative to the power generation we now use. Hydrogen fuel turbines will be perfected, carbon capture methods will be proven and the technology to make and separate the hydrogen gas will be proven. And there are other uses for the hydrogen gas such as clean transportation.

The future is *yours!* As engineers, chemists, physicists, economists, and biologists you will have lots of opportunities to contribute to the future. If we all work together, we can defeat the threat of global warming!

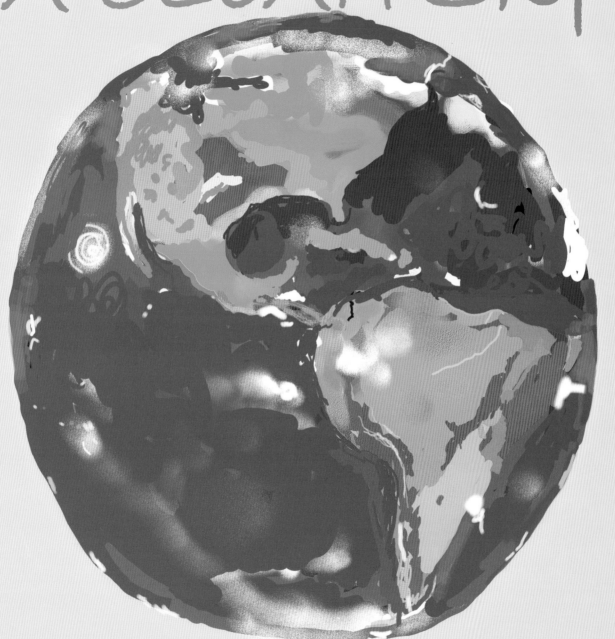

FUN FACTS

Fun Fact 1: Find out your Carbon Footprint!
What is a Carbon Footprint?

It is the amount of carbon dioxide your way of life adds to the atmosphere. It is based on things like your travel patterns and the amount of electricity you use at home.
Go to this web site:
http://www.bp.com/carbonfootprint
You can find out your carbon footprint!
You can also learn ways to decrease your carbon footprint.

Fun Fact 2: Why is it called "Greenland" if it is covered with ice?

Find Canada on a map. Look just to the right of Canada, and you will see a big island called Greenland. About 1,000 years ago, a famous explorer named Eric the Red first arrived there. Eric named the island "Greenland" because of the large number of trees and plants that were there, compared to Iceland, where he had been living before he found Greenland. He spent three years exploring Greenland, and then went home and brought a group of 25 ships back to southwest Greenland, forming a large colony.

Today Greenland is covered with ice, but it was not covered with ice when Eric the Red first went there in the year 981. Greenland is much colder today than it was then.

The colony survived for 400 years, but by around the year 1400, the weather had become so much colder that the colony was abandoned – some people died, and the rest left to live someplace warmer.

Fun Fact 3: What Do These Experts Do?

Agronomist: Agronomy is the study of field crops and soils. As an agronomist you might study how increased carbon dioxide levels or increased temperatures and a longer growing season might affect crop yields.

Biologist: Biology is the study of living things, such as plants and animals. As a biologist, you might study how different species come into existence, the interactions they have with each other, and how they might either benefit from or be harmed by the effects of global climate change.

Chemist: Chemistry is the study of the composition,

structure, and properties of substances, and the transformations they undergo. As a chemist, you might study the chemistry involved in various manufacturing processes, trying to devise new methods that will allow them to put fewer pollutants and greenhouse gases into the atmosphere and water.

Climatologist: Climatology is the study of climates, the weather over a long period of time. As a climatologist, you might study global climate change, determine the exact rate of change, and try to determine what factors (natural and man-made) are causing it.

Ecologist: Ecology is the study of the distribution and abundance of living organisms, and how that distribution and abundance are affected by interactions between the organisms and their environment. As an ecologist, you might study a particular animal to see if its population is going down or up, and learn what other plants and animals that particular animal depends on for food.

Economist: Economics is the study of the production, consumption, and distribution of goods and services. As an economist, you might study how global climate change will affect agriculture and manufacturing, and what steps might be taken to increase the positive effects, and to limit the negative effects.

Engineer: Engineering uses mathematics and the sciences to design, analyze, and construct works for practical purposes. As an engineer, you might invent a new process for clean manufacturing that puts fewer pollutants and greenhouse gases into the air.

Physicist: Physics is the science concerned with the discovery and understanding of the fundamental laws which govern matter, energy, space, and time. As a physicist, you might gain new knowledge that helps chemists, biologists, and engineers.

Glossary

Carbon Dioxide, sometimes called by its chemical formula, CO_2: A colorless, odorless gas that all animals and all people create when we exhale. It also is given off by burning, by volcanic eruptions, and other chemical reactions. Carbon dioxide is used by plants, leading to the vitally important "carbon cycle": plants take carbon dioxide from the atmosphere, absorb energy from sunlight, and release oxygen into the atmosphere; animals and humans take in that oxygen from the atmosphere by breathing, and release carbon dioxide; and this carbon dioxide released by animals and humans is then used by more plants. Without carbon dioxide, there would be no plant life on the Earth; without plant life, there could be no animal or human life. But there needs to be just the "right amount" of carbon dioxide to keep the cycle in balance.

Climate: The term for the average weather conditions of an area over many years.

Climate Change: The transition from a warmer climate to a cooler one, or from a cooler one to a warmer one. Climate change can be local (in just one area), or global (over the entire Earth). Climate change has taken place throughout the history of the Earth. Local climate change is usually caused by local factors (e.g., new mountain ranges, etc.). Scientists think that global climate change is mostly caused by small changes in the orbit and tilt of the Earth, which result in changes to the amount of sunlight that the Earth receives – as much as 25%!

Deforestation: This is when large areas of trees are cut down, either for agriculture or building development. Uncontrolled deforestation contributes to atmospheric greenhouse gases by removing the trees that take the carbon dioxide from the atmosphere and store it in their leaves and stems.

Fossil Fuel: "Fossil fuel" means things that were created by nature from decayed plants and microscopic animals (that's the "fossil" part) that we can burn for heat and energy (that's the "fuel" part). Their energy came originally from the sun, just like the energy in wood. Fossil fuels are nature's batteries – a way of storing energy from the sun. Examples of fossil fuels include oil, coal, and natural gas. Most of the energy used in the world today comes from fossil fuels.

Global Warming: The phase of climate change where the Earth's temperatures become, on average, warmer. **Global Cooling** is the opposite. In the past, there have been both periods of global warming and global cooling.

Greenhouse Effect: A term used to describe one of the most important mechanisms that keeps the Earth warm, wherein the light from the Sun warms the ground and the oceans, which give off infrared radiation, that in turn warms the atmosphere. This process doesn't work in the same way that a garden greenhouse does, but by the time this was understood, people had already gotten used to calling it the "Greenhouse Effect." The Greenhouse Effect is a term used to describe the effect when water vapor, carbon dioxide, and other "greenhouse gases" prevent the heat of the sun from escaping from the earth's atmosphere, and help thereby to keep the earth warm. Without the Greenhouse Effect, the Earth would be about 60 degrees colder than it is now! Water vapor is the most important greenhouse gas, followed by carbon dioxide. If we put a lot more carbon dioxide into the atmosphere by burning fossil fuel, it might raise the temperature of the Earth. Scientists are worried that industrial activity (burning fossil fuel), deforestation (cutting down forests, mostly in the tropics), and increased population will combine to increase the amount of carbon dioxide in the atmosphere.

Greenhouse Gas: These are the gases that produce the greenhouse effect. Water vapor is the most important greenhouse gas, followed by carbon dioxide. If we put a lot more carbon dioxide into the atmosphere by burning fossil fuels, it might raise the temperature of the Earth.

Hydrocarbon: A compound of hydrogen and carbon, found in fossil fuels like oil, natural gas, and coal. When burned as an energy source, the result is water vapor and carbon dioxide.

Hydroelectric Power: Power or electricity created by the force of water driving a generator.

Ice Age: Periods of time where the portion of the Earth covered by glacial ice was much larger than it is today. Scientists think that there are ice ages once every 40,000 to 100,000 years. Since the most recent ice age just ended (depending on the exact definition used, the most recent ice age ended at most 10,000 years ago, or is just ending right now), we are in a period of global warming caused by natural effects. Burning fossil fuel, cutting down tropical forests, and increasing our population may make global warming take place faster.

Industrialization: The period in the economic development of a nation when handicraft production becomes less significant than machine production.

Monsoon: A monsoon is a seasonal wind that blows from the southwest in India and nearby areas, and usually carries heavy rainfall with it.

Natural Gas: A fossil fuel that, when burned, creates less carbon dioxide than oil or coal.

Passive Solar Heating: A technique of using the sun directly to heat water or other substances.

Photosynthesis: The process whereby green plants take in carbon dioxide (mostly through their leaves) and water (mostly through their roots), and mix them together in the presence of sunlight and chlorophyll to produce glucose, which is utilized by the plant as energy. The plant releases oxygen as a part of this process; this is the source of the oxygen that keeps humans and animals alive.

Photovoltaic Cells: Devices that can turn sunlight directly into electricity.

Thermal Collectors: Devices that use the energy of sunlight to heat substances, like heating water in a passive solar heater for a swimming pool.

Turbines: A turbine is a device that uses the movement of air or water to turn a fan-like assembly; that turning motion can be used directly (to operate a machine, or to pump water), or can drive an electric generator (to generate electricity).

Visible and Infrared Radiation: Sunlight consists of electromagnetic energy. This energy comes in a mixture of different frequencies; think of it as broadcasting on several radio and television stations all at once. Some of the frequencies of sunlight are in the range that our eyes respond to, and are therefore called "visible radiation." Different frequencies of visible radiation generate different colors. Some of the frequencies of sunlight are *below* the range of frequencies that our eyes respond to; these are called "infrared." Some of the frequencies of sunlight are *above* the range of frequencies that our eyes respond to; these are called "ultraviolet."

Weather: The current conditions of temperature, humidity, wind, and precipitation. The pattern of weather over many years is called the *climate*.

Acknowledgements

Sincere appreciation to all of the Carson Hydrogen Power team members for sharing their knowledge and vision.

Special recognition to Susan Moore, Ben Moxham, Asteghik Khajetoorians and Tony Torres for lending their unique areas of expertise.

And many thanks to Quinlan Rau and Natalie Rau for providing a child's view.

hydrogen **energy**

clean energy for the future

bp

RIO TINTO

A Joint Venture between
BP Alternative Energy and Rio Tinto

BIOGRAPHIES

About the Author:

Robyn C. Friend is a singer, dancer, choreographer, and writer. She earned a Ph.D. in Iranian Linguistics at UCLA, and promptly launched a twenty-year career building spacecraft. She has written for both scholarly and popular publications on a wide variety of subjects, including folkloric dance, world music, linguistics, travel, and the exploration of Mars by balloon.

Judith Love Cohen is a Registered Professional Electrical Engineer with bachelor's and master's degrees in engineering from the University of Southern California and University of California, Los Angeles. She has written plays, screenplays, and newspaper articles in addition to her series of children's books that began with *You Can Be a Woman™ Engineer*.

About the Illustrator:

David Arthur Katz received his training in art education and holds a master's degree from the University of South Florida. He was a credentialed teacher in the Los Angeles Unified School District. His involvement in the arts has encompassed animation, illustration, playwriting, poetry, and songwriting. His art work is collected in various museums and his animations have played on PBS stations.